ALCOHOL FIEND TO SOBRIETY QUEEN

*25 Tips to Putting Down the Bottle and
Picking Up Your Crown*

CONNIE MCMILLAN

ALCOHOL FIEND TO SOBRIETY QUEEN
Copyright 2018 © ISBN
All rights reserved.
No part of this publication may be reproduced, distributed, or transmitted in any form or by any means, including photocopying, recording, or other electronic or mechanical methods, without the prior written permission of the publisher, except in the case of brief quotations embodied in critical reviews and certain other noncommercial uses permitted by copyright law.

From This

To This

Leaving No Woman Behind and Destroying the Curse of Alcohol Abuse, Use, and Dependency to Live a Life of Purpose on Purpose

This book is to help you ask yourself some questions regarding your relationship with alcohol. The hope is you make any necessary changes in your life by moving from self-destructive behavior to rebirthing. Alcohol might appear to be your friend, but how many people did you once think were your home girls only to find out later they were nothing but an undercover hater. That's exactly what a close relationship is with alcohol. It shows up like your bestie, cheerleader, supporter, courage juice, stress reliever, and so much more only to expose your darkest secrets and deepest pain and bringing the highest level of shame to your name. With a friend like that, who needs enemies.

For many years, alcohol ruled my entire being. Alcohol controlled everything from people, places, to things. Every time I drank I'd act of out character and wake up the next morning consumed with guilt and shame. I made promises not to do it again, but the next day, I was right back to the same old habits. The self-hatred I felt was so bad at times I could barely look in the mirror because of my damaged state of mind, which was a direct result of abusing alcohol.

Now, get ready because I'm about to share some of my most real yet surprising behavior while under the influence of alcohol. Maybe you can relate to my story, maybe you can't; either way, it's my truth, and I'm just grateful to have survived it.

I took my first drink as a child. I remember my favorite uncle asking me if I wanted some Kool-Aid. Of course, I didn't know at the time it was alcohol. I took a sip and swallowed it and said, "Uncle, that's not Kool-Aid." Who would've ever thought that would be my first taste of alcohol, but it certainly wasn't my last.

Contents

Tip 1 1
Tip 2 4
Tip 3 6
Tip 4 8
Tip 5 10
Tip 6 12
Tip 7 14
Tip 8 17
Tip 9 20
Tip 10 22
Tip 11 23
Tip 12 24
Tip 13 25
Tip 14 26
Tip 15 27
Tip 16 28
Tip 17 30
Tip 18 31
Tip 19 33
Tip 20 34
Tip 21 37

Tip 22 39

Tip 23 40

Tip 24 42

Tip 25 44

Tip 1

Putting down the bottle wasn't the easiest thing for me to do at all because I drank alcohol regularly. It was my boo, my best friend; honestly, LIT (Long Island Iced Tea) was my everything. In my mind, I used to believe it helped mend all the pain on the inside no one on the outside could see. I buried all the real pain, such as low self-esteem and negative thinking, on the inside. Surprisingly, I thought it also gave me courage to be bold enough to say and do the things I couldn't do when I was sober.

Putting down the bottle didn't come overnight; I had many failed attempts when I tried to do it on my own. But when I got sick and tired of the way alcohol was abusing me and went to the greatest source I knew for help, that's when things changed for me. One day, I took a long hard look at myself in the mirror for about 10 minutes. I looked horrible. My skin looked discolored, my eyes had lost all hope, and I had bags and dark circles under my eyes that no amount of makeup could hide. Also, my skin was just dry, ashy, and lusterless. I said to myself, "Connie, you need help because alcohol has you looking and acting a funky mess."

Really seeing myself in the mirror opened my eyes to the self-destructiveness I was bringing on myself. I needed to do something different because quitting for a couple of days or weeks on my own wasn't working for me. I needed to get this monkey off my back for good.

That's when I decided to take a different approach. I decided to take *everything* to God. I said, "Lord, this substance is going to *kill me*. I can't escape it on my own. I need you to help me. It's taken so many of my family members already, it's just too powerful for me to fight alone. I need you to take the taste out of my mouth, heart, and even out of my mind."

Although, I prayed to God, it didn't stop my flesh from wanting the very thing I was using regularly. The next day, I remember coming home from work I had to pass a liquor store. (You know, there's at least one on every other corner in the hood.) I started praying as I approached it, saying, "God, please help me not to go inside the liquor store, but it was as if my flesh had a mind of its very own. And it said, "You're going to get me what I want right now." It was so strong, and it wanted what it wanted: LIT. So, I obeyed my flesh and went inside the store and purchased a pint

I never needed company to drink; I was fine drinking at home alone. Whenever I would drink alone, those were the times I'd consume the most. I didn't have to worry about embarrassing myself in front anyone, and I was home so who could I harm. Some days it was a liter; other times, it was a gallon. In the end I'd feel worse than I felt before I started drinking. This night, I remember feeling like garbage because I thought God was through with me

One thing about alcohol: It takes you on an emotional roller coaster ride. I went home and poured myself a glass of LIT. I grabbed one of my wine glasses from my kitchen cabinet and put it inside the freezer for a few minutes to get a little frosty. About 10 minutes later, I removed the glass from the freezer sat it on the kitchen counter poured all the LIT inside the glass. (I can still smell the aroma of the alcohol as I write these words.)

I went in my bedroom, sat down on my bed, turned on the television, put the wine glass to my mouth, took a sip, began to quickly swallow, and almost choked to death. I started coughing like crazy. I couldn't understand what was happening. All I knew was I couldn't breathe for a few seconds. Once I could get some air into my lungs, I took another sip (I know, stupid, but it's the truth) and the *exact same experience happened*. I nearly choked to death except this time I dropped the wine glass on the floor, my eyes were watering because I felt as if I were going to die for what felt like eternity because I didn't have any air inside my lungs. I felt as if my life flashed before my eyes, and all I could do was think my life can't end this way.

Within the next few minutes, I got enough air into my lungs so I could breathe again, and all I could do was cry uncontrollably out to God thanking him for answering my prayer. I said, "God you saved me, you saved me. Thank you, Jesus. You knew I couldn't do this on my own." Today, I'm four years sober and counting, and I've never picked up another drink.

Tip 2

Identifying the problem is key to the success of your process of healing yourself from the inside out, without alcohol. My issue was low self-esteem, which started as a child. When I saw my reflection in the mirror, I saw black, ugly, and crooked teeth. It didn't help that I grew up in the 70s where light was right, and dark wasn't. As a result, I felt unattractive, stupid, and worthless.

I didn't read well as a child. Honestly, I hated reading, so I didn't do it. I remember my mom buying so many colorful books with animal pictures as her way to pique my interest. She would sit with me at the kitchen table for hours on any number of occasions helping me sound out the words in one of the books she purchased as we read together. But I just didn't want to do it. Because of this, I had to repeat the second grade. My mother didn't give up on me; she fought with me night after night and was very stern with me.

By the time I reached the fourth grade, the school administrators wanted to put me in a special education class, but my mother refused to allow them to label me. I remember her saying, "I know my child; she's not slow. She's just lazy and stubborn." My mother agreed to have the administrators set me up with additional resources such as one-on-one teaching outside of the regular classroom setting. I had this resource throughout fourth and fifth grades. By the time I entered sixth grade, things had improved so much I made the honor roll twice.

A mother's belief in her child makes a difference in so many ways. As I entered junior high school, I just knew my feelings about myself would change, especially since I was getting amazing grades for the first time ever in my life.

Sadly, my negative thoughts about myself didn't change because I was determined to dress up my appearance. This was certain to relieve me of my low self-esteem issue, *right?* Well at least that's what I thought. I was one of the flyest girls in junior high school rocking my Izod socks over my Guess jean pant legs (yup, I did that, don't judge me; it was 1984). You couldn't tell me one thing.

I had a name chain and the matching name ring, too. I was really starting to feel good about myself. People were really beginning to take notice. I felt good as if I fit in, too. This went on throughout high school. When I was a freshman, I had a gold tooth on the side of my mouth because there was no way I could get a gold tooth in the front of my mouth with crooked teeth. I wore bamboo earrings. Every new Polo jacket, shirt and shoes that came out I made sure to get them. I had an image to keep up, and I didn't care; I just wanted to be fly and for a very long time, I was somewhat happy.

This way of dressing went on even beyond high school. At this time, I upgraded to mink coats, red bottoms, designer watches and Gucci bags, but none of these things brought me the kind of satisfaction I felt when I had my "official" first drink as an adult.

Now, here I was over 30 years old still carrying baggage from my childhood. First, shopping was my choice to escape the mental and emotional pain I was battling only to later upgrade to abusing alcohol. The only thing shopping brought me was major credit card debt and some fake friends who I attracted as result my false representation of who I was.

Tip 3

Adjusting to life without alcohol will be difficult at first, especially in the beginning. Remember alcohol was the thing you used to escape pain so now it's up to you to lock in on your *why* (your reason) and God. These two, in my opinion, will be your greatest assets to the success of your journey. Your *why* will give you the strength you need to keep pushing forward. Remember I never took another drink after the choking episode. Well, that happened not only because I was afraid the third attempt would be my last strike, and I would die, but also God gave me *why*.

During the time I was drinking, I also had my current business, Cocktails with Chocolate, and I included alcohol in the bar service. Once God spared my life, he also told me, "Connie, I want you to revamp your business and take out the alcohol." Now, you must understand I couldn't see God's vision for my life or understand why he was telling me to remove the alcohol from my service.

That's why the reason for my response, "God, ain't nobody going to hire me for juice." God spoke again, "Connie, take the alcohol out of your service, and I will take you places you couldn't imagine." Who can top that? Nobody! God knew I had to include staying sober in my business as well as in future

He knew there was a need for my business. Although I couldn't see it, he knew it. Who can outdo God's plan for your life? Nobody can, and so I obeyed God's word, and he has kept his word. I have shared my story of surviving alcohol abuse, use, and dependency on platforms throughout the tri-state area (New York, New Jersey, and Connecticut) as well as with local magazines and News 12 Brooklyn, NY1, and other media.

I'm also the successful owner of Cocktails With Chocolate Non-Alcoholic Beverage Company, which offers mobile alcohol-free beverage service and bottled products for individuals to "Have a ball without alcohol" at all events. My company has shipped bottled products to Atlanta, Maryland, Florida, New York, Philadelphia, and Phoenix, just to name a few cities and states. This inspires me to look forward to doing business internationally.

Having a relationship with God keeps me grounded, humbled, and structured. I didn't know a lot about business prior to starting one, and I am forever learning with the help of God and coaches/mentors. Stand strong in your journey because there's a reason tied to it. You cannot let go because it's just the beginning of what's in store for you.

Tip 4

Dealing with the judgment: This is something you can't escape. People are going to talk about you whether you're doing good or bad so it's up to you how you respond to it. My first experience with judgment was shortly after I decided I wanted to share my story publicly, and I chose Facebook to do it. I didn't want to tell my story just to be telling it. I wanted there to be a great meaning why I was sharing it. The one-year anniversary of my mother's death was approaching (my mother died on January 16, 2014), and I wanted to do something in her honor.

Alcohol use, abuse, and dependency contributed to my mother's death but make no mistake about it, alcohol cannot nor will it *ever* take away from the *amazing* queen she was and will forever be in my life. On January 16, 2015, I shared my story for the very first time in detail of how I had battled with alcohol use, abuse, and dependency privately for more than 10 years.

I shared with my friends and family about how I had used alcohol to mask my pain only to find more pain in the end. Lots of people expressed shock mostly because the life I was living via social media showed no signs of alcohol abuse. They saw a woman who was always out partying and enjoying life.

I can still recall the comments people made mostly positive, supportive, thanking me for sharing. But of course, negativity is real, too. The negative comment that stuck out the most was when a young lady sent me a private message that said, "OMG, Connie, I didn't know you were an alcoholic. What happened to you? What did you do when you were drinking?" You must understand there will be two types of audiences you'll encounter: those who want help and your story will be the seed planted to help start their fertilization process. Then, there is the other audience who will just want to be nosy and get up in your business just to have something to gossip about.

So of course, this person who was asking me all these questions "privately" did so thinking she was protecting me. I wasn't ashamed of my actions that's why I chose to share them publicly myself. Her asking me these questions "privately" wasn't for my protection it was "her" protection.

It's possible she didn't want others to know what she was asking me. But make no mistake about; it she wasn't protecting me. I simply replied, "You weren't supposed to know I was abusing and using alcohol at that time in my life. I wasn't ready to expose myself, and thank God, he didn't allow me to be put in a position to be exposed at that point in my life. As for my sharing in greater detail my acts involving alcohol use, abuse, and dependency with you, how will it help you? Are you battling with substance abuse?"

When you recognize whom you're speaking to, be direct with them. As for her response, I never got one from her. The point is this: Some people will genuinely be concerned about your past life, and others will just want to be nosy. Discover who they are and handle them accordingly.

Tip 5

Moving past the fear of leaving the crew behind can be one of the most frightening and hardest experiences in life. Trust me, I get it! You're not only fearful of leaving your old friends; you're afraid of what they will say, think, and share about your decision. And you're concerned whether you'll ever make new ones.

My thoughts were the same. How will I adjust? What if I don't adjust? Why would anyone want to be friends with me now? Oh, the list goes on. I used to believe that loyalty to my friends was the most important thing in my life. Even if that meant staying at the level I was on, costing me my own true happiness and freedom.

It wasn't until I heard these words, "You become the result of the five closest people you spend the most time with." These words caused me to wake up and get my life together. I had to face my truth. I wasn't surrounding myself with the best company. All we did was party, shop, get drunk, meet guys (have intercourse with them), travel to a few states only to party and do the same things all over again. We never went to the library, researched jobs together, took professional training courses, etc. Everything we did involved alcohol. Not to mention how often we couldn't remember what we did the next morning. I was the smartest person in the crew. And that isn't a compliment to myself by any means; that just means I was okay with not growing, okay with being mediocre. I was good with wasting my life on partying and getting drunk.

I'm not trying to bash my old crew at. All these women weren't horrible people, but I always knew my life was meant for more. I knew I had a greater destiny. I was the best player on the worst team. Meaning: I surrounded myself with people who needed me, yet I needed so much more help myself.

Tip 6

Finding a new crew will happen sooner than you know it. The most important thing is that you safeguard your own environment when it comes to alcohol use. You get to decide what kind of company is best for you. And that includes people who respect your right to choose an alcohol-free life. Finding individuals who don't drink alcohol at all isn't hard to do. There are many social events you can attend such as meetups on and offline with individuals who don't drink alcohol. There are events you can attend all year long, as well, not just on holidays.

The following are some of the social event outlets you can use (these are just suggestions) Sober Grid, Sober Movement, Sober Is Sexy (online), Cocktails With Chocolate Annual Sober Party (once a year offline), and Big Vision Community (offline) If these don't fit your personality, you can always attend events at your church or start your own social events surrounding fun and sobriety.

As you go along your journey, you will meet some of the most amazing people in life. I believe that once you make a healthy choice to release toxic relationships from your life, God finds a way to fulfill that space with individuals to help get you to the next stage in your life journey.

Always remember elevation requires separation. I have made so many new friends via social media who have changed my life forever. Among the many motivators, my favorites are Eric Thomas (ET), one of the top motivational speakers in the world, and Koereyelle Dubose an incredible speaker, author, and female entrepreneur who is helping to inspire, educate, and empower women to live a life they love. Your new crew is waiting with open arms to receive you. Get ready!

Tip 7

Removing the old negative thoughts was probably one of the most challenging parts of my journey. There would be days upon days of negative thoughts that would torment me while living in my new environment. I literally moved to another city and state: from Brooklyn, New York to East Orange, New Jersey. Honestly, it wasn't even my choice; this was all God's doing.

Often, I questioned whether the decision to relocate was the right one. It got so bad I would question God, "What was the point in you bringing me out here? I don't know anyone. I hate the neighborhood, I want to go back to Brooklyn." It's common to want to go back to the place of comfort when discomfort is all around you even when the comfortable place you left is the place that caused you the most harm.

I had the right to be fearful because God was exposing me to an unfamiliar place. It wasn't perfect. But neither was I. God had placed me in this new environment for a specific reason: to get my undivided attention. Yes, the negative thoughts were there attacking me mentally and emotionally, but it was in those moments I had time to remember that where I am now is much better than where I came from.

One day, when I was going through my mental, emotional, and ungrateful moments, God shared this with me: "***Connie, when you first saw this apartment, it looked nothing like the photo on Craigslist. In the photo, the apartment was beautiful with shiny wood floors, freshly painted, a sunken living room as well as beautiful glazed garden bathtub.***

"However, when you arrived to view the apartment, it looked like it had been through war. The wood floors were dull, it needed a fresh coat of paint, and the garden tub was dirty, and the exterior was peeling. You were scared and unsure whether you should leave a security deposit, but you did. And because of your obedience to move forward regardless of what you saw with your natural eyes, when you returned on the move-in day, the apartment was transformed into the photo you saw on Craigslist."

God was showing me, "Connie, when you first arrived in New Jersey you were in bad shape just like the apartment so it's okay that you may *not* understand why I brought you to New Jersey right now, but when I'm through with you, however long it takes, you too will look brand-new just like this new apartment I brought you into."

Please know this: I showed up a funky mess, broken, bruised, doubtful, fearful, and abused, but it was just for the benefit of God to begin a new work inside me. I'm seeing the promises of his word that says, "For I know the plans I have for you," declares the Lord, "plans to prosper you and not to harm you, plans to give you hope and a future." (Jeremiah 29:11)

I don't care what thoughts remind you of your past, know that you're on your journey of survival now for a reason. It doesn't matter how much clean time you have because God's clean time isn't your clean time. Your one day of clean time in the eyes of God can equal months or years. Speak words of power into your life when old negative thoughts try to detour you because you're somebody's solution.

Tip 8

You'll never reach your destiny locked up in a tomb. For so many years, I thought my battle with alcohol was solely about me. My struggle, my dependency, even my abuse. But the truth of the matter is it wasn't just my battle I was fighting because so many relatives of mine had battled this very same fight. Unfortunately, they lost their battle, and they passed this battle on to me. I didn't ask for this battle, but I know I was specifically chosen to defeat it!

See, the demonic spirit of alcohol abuse, use, and dependency started long before I was born. My mother drank, my aunts, uncles, and grandfather all drank alcohol. They may not have all abused alcohol, but it was a part of their environment. They used it to release some form of emotion and/or to mask pain. This spirit attached itself to my bloodline before I was even in my mother's womb. In fact, alcohol use, abuse, and dependency affects many other bloodlines, and it can wipe out purpose, destiny, happiness, joy, confidence, wisdom, etc.

I felt locked in a tomb for many years, believing the very lies I told myself as a child: You're ugly, black, your teeth are crooked, you don't read well, you got left back in the second grade, *you're just not worthy*. The negativity started in my mind early, which then led me to want to use alcohol as my way to release my emotional and mental pain. This tomb imprisoned my mind for a long time, just as it had my relatives. It led them too to believe alcohol was their friend, their problem solver, stress reliever only to find themselves in a worse state and, ultimately, dying.

When God answered my prayer, that was him saying, "Connie, it's your turn to step up, release yourself from the tomb of alcohol abuse, use, and dependency. God unlocked the door, but it was my job to walk through it. It's my job to fight for my territory. It's my job to fight for the future of my family as well as other families. It's my job to understand that my adversity created an opportunity.

I ask you the following questions: What thing in your life has you locked in a tomb? Does it have you believing you'll never get free? Does it have you believing you're not strong enough? Does it have you believing this is just how your family deals with pain? Has it already taken the lives of your family members? If so, it's your turn to be freed; it's your turn to be the answer to the problem. Now is the time to release yourself from this tomb so you can release your bloodline from the generational curse! *Fight for your future because you are the answer*!

Tip 9

Create a safe space for yourself. The unfortunate truth of the matter is alcohol will always be a part of this world, probably forever, because it's a billion-dollar industry regardless of how many individuals' lives it destroys. Knowing what to do should you ever have to be around alcohol is vital.

Let's say the company you work for has an annual holiday party or your family member has a yearly July 4th barbeque. We both know alcohol will be plentiful. Being prepared is so important when you're on your journey to living an alcohol-free life. Here are some of the ways I maintained my sobriety journey for the past four years and counting. First, I decide whether the event is a priority or not. Attending your family function isn't necessarily mandatory. Neither is attending the company annual Christmas party. But let's just say for argument's sake you must attend these kinds of events. Having an alcohol-free beverage on hand will ultimately be your best option.

No soldier goes to war without a plan on how to defeat the enemy. Being prepared is your best option. Here are two suggestions: Carry your own nonalcoholic beverage let others know it's for your use only. You can also bring two beverages, one for your personal use and the other so guests can drink. If you have a considerate, understanding host, he or she will provide a choice of nonalcoholic beverages.

If you want something more appealing, please visit my website www.cocktailswithchocolate.com to order one of my amazing bottled products: Apricot Nectar Bellini, Party All the Time, or Sweet Jesus. These are my signature bottled products created just so you can be prepared for any social occasion that alcohol will be present, and you can "Get Lit and Remember It." What's most important is don't ever go into any event unprepared because you leave yourself open to attack, setback, and/or defeat. If you feel weakness sneaking up, get out! You don't owe anyone an explanation other than yourself.

Tip 10

Guarding your mind, body, and spirit is your way of helping to heal yourself mentally, physically, and spiritually. Reading is a wonderful way I guard my mind to rid myself of the any-old mess. It's my way of discarding old unused, worn out, no longer needed thoughts and reserving space in my mind for information that adds to my life like the Bible, affirmations, motivational books, videos, and audios.

My body is my temple, and it's my job to see to it I take care of it. I've done enough damage to it in my past, so eating healthy, drinking lots of water, and exercising are some of the ways that help repair the past damage. Spirituality for me is the icing on the cake.

You see mind and body are the like the oil and flour (and eggs and sugar) you add when you bake a cake. But the baking pan holds it all together. Without the pan, the other ingredients only serve a limited purpose. Putting all of them together and baking a delicious cake takes your taste buds to an entirely new level. That's exactly what spirituality will do for your walk on this journey. God is the icing on the cake; you'll see a difference in your life immediately.

Tip 11

Remembering your *why* prevents you from falling off course and getting distracted and losing sight of your goal of sobriety. Understand what you stand to lose if you go back to drinking. Those are the thoughts you must keep in your mind. My initial why was to honor my mother, and it still is. However, my why has evolved into being an example to young girls and women in my family as well as women and girls around the world to see what's possible with sobriety.

Many women who suffer privately as well as publicly with alcohol abuse, use, and dependency need to see what lies at the end of coming out of alcohol abuse. I'm the result of what's possible with sobriety. It's now my obligation to share my story every chance I get, every detail—the good, bad, and the ugly—to inspire individuals to know if Connie can fight this battle and overcome it daily, then my life is just as valuable and worth fighting for, too. I am just one person standing up sharing my story and running this race, and the torch must pass on to as many people as possible to continue to share the possibilities with sobriety.

Tip 12

God can take total disaster and turn it into victory. I am a living, walking, breathing testament of what God can do it when you ask for his help. When my mother died, we had four other deaths in our family that very same year. It was like every other couple of months someone in my family died. I hadn't even begun to heal from the loss of my mom before I found out yet another one of my relatives had also died. To make matters worse, at the time of my mother's death there was very cold weather with temperatures so low, the ground was frozen so they couldn't bury her body. Arrangement were made for her body to put in a mausoleum temporarily. My mother was officially buried March.

I remember feeling that now we can bury our queen properly, but going back to the burial was even more painful. Seeing my mother's body go into the ground was the hardest thing I've had to do, but also in that moment, I realized I had to fight, share, tell my story about the dangers of alcohol abuse, use, and dependency. To be honest I couldn't have written this book had I not lost my mother for two reasons: I was so busy trying to protect the family secret, and second, I wasn't strong enough nor did I have the positive attitude I do now. I understand my mother's death put the wheels in motion for me to get moving and tell my truth to help someone else find healing and do the same in their family.

Tip 13

A support circle is definitely necessary. Choosing to be around the right company will be your best decision. Your support can come in various forms, professionally and/or personally (family, friends, church, etc.). Having individuals in your corner to be your additional strength is a bonus. These are people who can motivate you and keep you going when the temptation to drink tries to creep in.

On the other side of the coin: That means you have to drop all the negative Nancys, doubtful and complacent people who try to take up your time saying and doing things that don't add value to your life. Don't make time for them. Why? Because you're on your own journey, and you can't afford to add pressure on yourself and jeopardize your life and possibly fall off the wagon.

Have you ever flown in an airplane, and the flight attendant announces what to do in case of an emergency? They always tell you to secure your oxygen mask first before securing anyone else's? Having a circle of friends who can and will add value to your life are the individuals whose oxygen mask is secure. That's why they can assist you. Your surrounding yourself in a positive environment is you securing your oxygen mask for yourself.

Tip 14

Share your story. Don't let fear punk you by not sharing your story when led to share it. Because sharing your story not only helps continue to strengthen and empower you, it empowers the audience you share your story with. Keeping it all to yourself is a form of selfishness. Sharing it for the first time will be hard, and you may be incredibly nervous; actually, you will be. But think of the lives you'll change because of sharing your truth. Think of the release you'll give yourself when you tell your entire story.

I know you might not see it now, but remember this, things happen for us not to us. Whenever I tell my story publicly, I still get nervous because all eyes are on me. But I get past my emotions and say, "Connie, someone else needs to hear your story. They need to hear your voice even as it quivers; they need to know there's someone out there who has gone through what they're now dealing with. They need to know they can get through this struggle. They need to know it's all working together for their good. Your sharing your story gives individuals the opportunity to become just as bold as you are. *Don't let Fear Punk You; Share Your Story.*

Tip 15

Expect both negative and positive feedback from strangers. Negative feedback usually comes from people who aren't as bold to share their truths. You must remember this; people who speak negativity wish they could be as bold as you. Because they chose not to be, they see negativity as their only option. Don't take it personally; pray for them.

The positive comments will come more often in the form of letters, social media, etc. Positive feedback will be from people who can relate to some or all your journey. Nearly every event I attend or even speak at, I'm always approached afterwards by someone feeling led to share their experience with me. That's because of my willingness to share my story regardless of how uncomfortable it makes others feel.

The individuals who listen to your story, every good, bad, and ugly part, will view you as one of the strongest, most courageous, and transparent individuals alive. You will become their hero. Strangers will hug you, shake your hand and take a picture with you because you'll inspire them to start their journey of survival or something else they've been wanting to do for a very long time.

Tip 16

We are who we attract. The very things we're holding on to are the very things we must release. It could be people, places, and or things. I was holding on to the "fashion queen" label, believing buying expensive items would raise my low self-esteem and make me feel good about myself. Nope, didn't work. I attracted company that dressed as I did, but that didn't help me, either. I partied and drank a lot, and as a result, I attracted the same kinds of individuals. I attracted all the wrong relationships, including my ex-husband. Within me was the hurt, pain, brokenness, low self-esteem, emptiness, feelings of longing, wanting acceptance, etc., which is why I kept hurting myself repeatedly.

    I never took the time to address the problem and heal it properly. Whenever there was pain in my life, I often masked it with alcohol, not realizing it would lead me to more pain. One evening I remember, I was feeling unattractive and just needing something to lift my spirits. Instead of finding out why I felt this way, I decided to go out to a club by myself. Here I was already in a fragile state, and I decided to put myself in harm's way. (At the time, I didn't see that way.)

    Of course, I drank a lot that night. Soon after, I remember feeling good, sexy, and confident after about two drinks. Later that evening, I met a guy who I danced with, and he bought me more drinks. I went back to his apartment and had sex with him that same night. We never spoke again, and I couldn't even tell you his first name. Looking back, I'm grateful I wasn't killed.

    The point I'm making is this: You must heal the pain within rather than try to mask it believing it will go away by itself, because it won't. If not, you will attract everything that's within you only to have it expand into something greater and more painful.

Tip 17

Keep the promises you make to yourself because they'll be the most valuable words you'll come to know. We hear the words we speak first so don't use them casually. Let them be impactful, life-changing, world-shifting, and action-driven. Here are a few you can say and write down: I am powerful, I am beautiful, I am worthy, I am smart, I am greater than my past, I am a positive example for all women and men, I am destroying the generational curses in my family, I am no longer a victim of alcohol abuse, I am no longer bound to my past, I am leaving a positive legacy for my family to follow.

On the following line, create one additional promise of your own: I am_____. Hold yourself accountable by signing this declaration to yourself. Sign here_____. Be sure to tear this sheet out of this book and hang these words someplace you'll see them daily.

Tip 18

False beliefs about alcohol: It helps you relax, boosts your confidence, deals with the pain of life, makes you feel socially acceptable and more. The truth is it will all come at a great cost financially, mentally, physically, and emotionally. For example, someone who sees an alcohol ad that shows a fabulous lifestyle with people partying and enjoying life on a yacht is very attractive, especially when everyone dresses in their best and look as if they belong on the front cover of an *Essence* or *Vogue* magazine.

But what happens once someone who views this ad tries to make it their reality? What about the individual(s) who's already battling alcohol abuse privately? How are they to know what's real from what's false about alcohol use and abuse? What happens when the individual consumes this poison in the ad in their real-life, thinking and believing they have nothing to fear, alcohol is here?

So, they begin drinking daily, weekly, or monthly. What happens when it gets so bad they become dependent, and their life isn't recognizable anymore? Their finances are in ruins, their family members are concerned, their physical appearance has changed as well as their behavioral patterns, all because of the false images associated with the alcohol advertisement.

The ads on television, magazines, subways, and even billboards are all created for one purpose: **To Make Money By Any Means Necessary**. Even at the cost of your losing your family and or your life. The alcohol companies don't care about you after they have your money. They care about what you can do for them financially. That's why the images are beautiful and appealing. The ad companies' job is to evoke an emotion within you. It's called marketing for a reason: It's designed to get the sale at any cost!

Tip 19

Resource are available to help you not harm you. Today, we live in a world where you can get almost anything with just a click of a button. Technology has spoiled us rotten. You can order food, pet services, laundry, even a baby sitter by just clicking an app on your phone. I'm guilty by the way. These options are for a reason: to provide a variety to customers who might not want to go the traditional route of going into the establishment.

Let's face it the traditional way of doing things is the past. Modern technology is faster, easier, and much more convenient. The same options are available for you when it comes to resources regarding sobriety. Gone are the days where you must go the traditional route of attending meetings.

The way I gained my sobriety was outside the "norm." As I've shared earlier, I did it God's way not AA. This is no disrespect to AA because they're responsible for helping many people gain sobriety. However, there are options when it comes to taking the first step to starting your journey of sobriety. There is inpatient, outpatient, group meetings both online and offline, private counseling, professional programs, etc. Making the first step is your best move ever.

Tip 20

10 Commandments of sobriety: These can serve as a daily, inspirational reminder.

1. Refuse to receive or believe anything negative about yourself. Tell old corrupt thoughts goodbye, you don't live here anymore. God has begun a new thing inside of you. See 2 Corinthians: 5:17.
2. Surround yourself with likeminded people. Stay connected to sobriety groups as well as individuals who think positively and produce positive results. See Proverbs 13:20.
3. Stay physically active. Choose running, power walking, yoga, spin class, kick boxing, or whatever piques your interest. This helps to burn off those extra pounds that come from drinking and increases your energy level and is wonderful way to maintain your temple (body). See Romans 12:1.
4. Clean house of those who were your drinking buddies or those who encouraged you to drink. Avoid anyone or anything that may tempt you to return to the prison life you've just escaped. Avoid it like the plague. Just as you're reconstructing your mind and body you will need to reconstruct relationships to live a successful, sober life. See Leviticus 20:26.
5. Make the weekend a time for appreciation rather than celebration. Spend this time with those who support your new life of sobriety by creating amazing memories with them. It can include playing cards, board games, getting a manicure, going to an amusement park, movies, spa day, or having a family picnic. (Don't forget to bring your nonalcoholic beverage.) See Luke 12:34.

6. Go after your passion with everything in you. Remember this is your new beginning; don't waste a minute of it. Philippians 4:13.

7. Don't pick up a drink under *any* circumstances. Keep your eyes forward. Things in your rearview mirror become smaller than they truly are. See Philippians 3:13-14.

8. Over time, your urges will decrease, and it will get easier to live as the Sober Queen you're destined to be. See Acts 3:21.

9. Remember your why and allow it to overtake the very core of you mentally, physically, and emotionally. Each new day, be proud of how far you've come and give recognition to yourself every day, week, and month. See Isaiah 43:19.

10. Stay connected and remain strong in your sobriety. You're an answer for someone's problem: Walk like it, talk like it, plan like it. See Psalms 32:8.

36

Tip 21

Take the test: The purpose of this test is for you to examine your relationship with alcohol to see how it alters your behavior and or possibly those around you.

Be honest and ask yourself these simple questions and answer them:

1. What's my relationships with alcohol? a. Stress reliever b. takes the edge off, c. other
2. Why do you drink it?

_____

3. When do you drink it?

_____

4. How much do you drink? A little (a glass) A lot (3 glasses) Turn up Queen (can't stop; won't stop)
5. How often do you drink? Once a day, once a week, more
6. When do you drink?

_____

7. What is your behavior like because of drinking? Aggressive, happy/sad, promiscuous
8. Do people say you're different when you drink? If so, what are some of the things they say about you? Examples: You're more likeable, You're unlikeable, You're funny, etc.

_____

9. Do your friends and or family members promote your drinking? Yes or No

10. Have you ever done something you regretted because of your drinking? Yes or No.

Tip 22

Create a legacy for your family. Alcohol doesn't have to destroy any more lives in your family. But it will if you don't stand up and fight for it. You can become the one in your family to say: Enough is enough. I won't allow this substance to be the guest of honor any longer at any more events held with my family. No more will it be invited as the #1 beverage choice. No longer will I be present to deceive and destroy my sisters, brothers, children, grandchildren, cousins, aunts, and uncles, etc.

No longer will I make excuses for the person in my family who uses alcohol as a way of escaping past and current pain. Start speaking up, use your voice as the instrument for doing good. Speak up about the effects it's had on all family and friends you know. Staying quiet gives life to the toxic substance use within your family by allowing alcohol to have free range and destroy more lives in your bloodline now and many generations to come. Exposing this "family secret" will bring forth new life, healing, and power. Get honest about why you're choosing to live a life free of alcohol use. Remember it's for the legacy of your family.

Tip 23

Alcohol is a depressant not a stimulant. Although your reason for drinking alcohol could be to feel better, the fact is you won't. Ever wonder why after a night of drinking with the crew you feel moments when you're down or even depressed. It's because alcohol has a sedative effect, which means at high doses, it depresses the brain.

At lower doses, alcohol can act as if it's a stimulant, making you feel high and chatty, but that's a lie, and you'll find that out the next day. Drinking too much alcohol at once can lead to "drowsiness, respiratory depression (breathing becomes slow, shallow, or stops entirely), coma, or even death," according to https://www.alcohol.org.nz/alcohol-its-effects/about-alcohol/what-is-alcohol.

Tip 24

When you know better, you do better, and it starts with knowing how alcohol affects your body from the inside out. Drinking too much—on a single occasion or over time—can take a serious toll on your health. Here's how alcohol can affect your body:

Read these effects from the National Institutes of Health (https://www.niaaa.nih.gov/alcohol-health/alcohols-effects-body)
Brain:
Alcohol interferes with the brain's communication pathways and can affect the way the brain looks and works. These disruptions can change mood and behavior and make it harder to think clearly and move with coordination.
Heart:
Drinking a lot over a long time or too much on a single occasion can damage the heart, causing problems, including:
- Cardiomyopathy—Stretching and drooping of heart muscle
- Arrhythmias—Irregular heartbeat
- Stroke
- High blood pressure

Liver:
Heavy drinking takes a toll on the liver and can lead to a variety of problems and liver inflammations, including:
- Steatosis, or fatty liver
- Alcoholic hepatitis
- Fibrosis

- Cirrhosis

Pancreas:

Alcohol causes the pancreas to produce toxic substances that can eventually lead to pancreatitis, a dangerous inflammation and swelling of the blood vessels in the pancreas that prevents proper digestion.

Tip 25

Forgiveness starts from within, and it brings forth new life. I am writing this letter to the old Connie,

You did a lot of horrible things to hide the person you were created to be. Although God hand-crafted you, you didn't embrace her. Instead, you did things to cover her and harm her. In doing so, you abused her, you shamed her and brought her lots of pain as well as to others close to you. You put hope in people and things believing they would validate you. You put them first and her last too many times to count, thinking they were the answer instead of trusting the only reliable source, God.

You sold your body and soul for a taste of alcohol for over 10 years every time you consumed it. You stole money from your mother just to feed the brokenness so deeply buried within you, yet the act of your dishonesty, theft, and mistrust hurt her more than the pain you were trying to shield. All these things you did because of the pain, hurt, deep scars that were living inside you that nobody ever saw. You hid it from everyone believing you could handle it all by yourself, only to learn that was a lie.

I want to apologize for the pain and shame I brought to your name, Connie. Today, I am stronger, wiser, healed, and seeking God as my number one source. I'm so grateful to my mother (before she passed), God, and me for forgiving me. Looking ahead, you have a destiny that's calling your name, which is to show women around the world sobriety and to heal from the inside out and live a life of purpose on purpose.

www.ingramcontent.com/pod-product-compliance
Lightning Source LLC
Chambersburg PA
CBHW051949160426
43198CB00013B/2364